Mastering the Art of Swedish Death Cleaning

A Practical Workbook to Declutter, Organize, Revitalize Your Home and Life and Embrace the Essence of What Truly Matters

Maria D. Garland

Table of Contents

Introduction

When I first came across the term "Swedish death cleaning," I must admit that a rather intense image formed in my mind—an all-night decluttering spree that leaves you utterly exhausted, akin to feeling near death. Little did I know that there's much more to it.

I read "The Gentle Art of Swedish Death Cleaning" by Margareta Magnusson to explore this further. The author, aged between 80 and 100, sheds light on the Swedish cultural tradition of tidying up and settling affairs before passing away. In Swedish, this practice is referred to as "döstädning." It's viewed as a natural phase of life, often undertaken around age 65. However, this approach can be beneficial at any age, provided you adopt the right perspective.

While many focus on leaving behind a financial legacy, the book highlighted a pivotal realization for me. Whatever we leave behind becomes a barrier that hinders our loved ones' grieving and healing process. Our desire is for fond memories of us to prevail, yet leaving a trail of clutter and possessions complicates that outcome.

Why We Tend to Accumulate and Hoard Possessions

First, a "clutter instinct" is driven by the need to feel abundant and not deprived. Second, a "hoarding instinct" stems from a survival mindset—keeping items in anticipation of emergencies. Lastly, our fear of death and vanishing memories contribute to our attachment to our belongings.

When adopting the Swedish death cleaning method, a mindset shift is imperative. The pivotal question is:

"Will anyone find greater happiness if I retain this item?"

Often, the things we hold dear are only meaningful to us. They might not hold the same significance for others. As your loved ones come across your belongings, will they comprehend why you kept them? Will they grasp the stories behind these items?

The ultimate goal of Swedish death cleaning is to minimize the burden on those we leave behind, fostering a legacy of cherished memories rather than clutter.

One of the most poignant aspects of the Swedish death cleaning method is its ability to share cherished memories with loved ones during one's lifetime. It provides the opportunity to explain why specific items were treasured and offers a chance to convey the intent behind gifting certain items as part of an inheritance. This openness and communication are truly beautiful elements of this approach.

There are three distinct approaches to Swedish death cleaning. The first method is the most private and leisurely. It involves sifting through your possessions at your own pace, donating or selling unused items, and identifying those special items that hold a resounding "yes" to the previously mentioned question. These selected items are then labeled or accompanied by notes elucidating their significance, history, and even the intended recipient upon your passing.

The second approach resonates with the scenario many individuals find themselves in when they're downsizing due to a move from a long-inhabited house to a smaller residence, such as an apartment or assisted living. This process usually entails gathering family members together to make swift decisions about belongings. However, this method can be overwhelming, pressuring individuals to decide under duress. Memories flood back all at once, making clear thinking a challenge.

Gifting

The third approach involves gradually gifting items to friends and family over several years. Swedish death cleaning isn't solely about sentimental mementos; practical items can also be part of the process. Consider items like furniture that may not fit in your new space but could be cherished by someone else. This method allows for a smoother transition, a gradual sharing of possessions that brings joy both to you and the recipients. It might even provide solace amid the journey.

Nevertheless, it's crucial to avoid projecting guilt onto the new owners of these items. While certain items hold immense personal value, their significance may not resonate similarly with someone else. Each person's connection to belongings varies, and that's perfectly acceptable. Ultimately, the essence of Swedish death cleaning lies in thoughtful consideration, open communication, and an intention to simplify and enhance the lives of those you care about most.

One noteworthy aspect is the presence of personal, deeply private items we may conceal. These are the "for your eyes only" possessions, such as private journals or sensitive photographs. Imagining our family stumbling upon such items after our passing might be discomforting. Considering this, it might be wise to contemplate disposing of these items beforehand to spare our loved ones from an unexpected discovery.

While Swedish death cleaning shares some commonalities with decluttering techniques like the KonMari method, it ascends to a distinct level. This approach holds a particular sense of nobility, transcending personal benefits by considering the impact on those we hold dear. By lightening the load for our loved ones, this practice attains a heightened significance beyond mere tidying. It's not merely about letting go of possessions; it's a thoughtful process of bestowing a legacy and easing the transition for others.

Approaching Swedish death cleaning should be a cherished phase in one's life. It's an opportunity to cradle items, relive the memories they evoke, and truly appreciate the richness of your life's journey. By framing it this way, it becomes a profoundly meaningful endeavor, enhancing your understanding of your experiences.

Let's dive into it!

Chapter 1: Discover the Gentle Art of Swedish Death Cleaning

'The Gentle Art of Swedish Death Cleaning.' by Margareta Magnusson offers a refreshing approach to downsizing.

At its core, 'death cleaning' involves evaluating all your belongings and making deliberate decisions about their future. As Magnusson eloquently says, "Death cleaning is going through all my belongings and deciding how to get rid of things I do not want anymore. Just look around you. Several of your things have probably been there for so long that you do not even see or value them anymore."

This concise yet insightful book spans just over a hundred pages, brimming with organizational and downsizing wisdom, interwoven with personal anecdotes. It feels as if Magnusson embarked on her own downsizing journey, documenting challenges and innovative solutions that have culminated in this book.

Magnusson, who places herself within the age bracket of eighty to a hundred, suggests that downsizing is ideal in one's 60s when energy is still abundant. However, you'll find valuable decluttering insights whether you're in your 30s, 40s, 50s, or beyond.

Magnusson offers thoughtful 'because' phrases to broach the subject sensitively. She furnishes examples of phrases that gently nudge parents toward downsizing. For instance, you might inquire, "You have many cherished possessions. Have you considered their future? Does your current abundance bring you joy? Could life become simpler and less taxing with fewer belongings accumulated over the years? Can we collaborate gradually to minimize the load?"

Magnusson advises tackling storage spaces first—attics, basements, garages, and storage units. Her rationale is that items tucked away and forgotten likely hold little significance. Throughout the book, a recurring theme stresses the importance of not burdening the next generation with a surplus of possessions. Rather, the aim is to leave behind a sense of order instead of an overwhelming accumulation for future generations.

Magnusson also presents a recommendation: avoiding the commencement of downsizing with a dive into old letters and photographs. She astutely points out that the nostalgic allure of these items can hinder efficient downsizing. The temptation to get lost in memories and reflections might derail the intended progress for the day. This counsel speaks volumes, preventing sentimental detours from derailing the downsizing mission.

The book systematically delves into specific categories, like the kitchen, clothing, and collectibles. Magnusson recounts seeking advice on selling items, collaborating with estate agents for auctions, and discovering inventive avenues for parting with possessions. She outlines her experiences, from identifying agencies interested in particular items to engaging friends and family members in adopting cherished belongings. An underlying principle she underscores is the significance of attaching personal stories to these items before they transition to new hands. This practice of bestowing possessions while still alive, accompanied by their stories, emerges as a pivotal point. Rather than leaving the narrative behind objects to posthumous auctions, she champions sharing stories and transferring items to their future custodians.

Amidst the personal anecdotes and life stories, the book also offers practical advice. For instance, during her own downsizing process within her home, she designated distinct rooms with labels: "Keep," "Move," "Give Away," and "Throw Away." These physical spaces facilitated organization, allowing her to categorize items accordingly. These designated spaces enabled her to streamline her thought process about where each item belonged. Moreover, she employed detailed labeling, specifying where an item was headed and its intended recipient. Keeping a well-maintained list of these items ensured preparedness when the opportunity arose to gift them to someone.

Passing on Gifts

One aspect that often proves challenging for individuals is parting with items received as gifts.

How does one navigate the emotional hurdle of letting go of something given with care?

The author addresses this issue thoughtfully. She suggests that when she bestows a present upon someone, she acknowledges that it may not remain with that person indefinitely. After all, who truly keeps track of every gift we've given away? Things tend to break or become obsolete over time. She emphasizes that the essence of gratitude should be associated with the act of receiving a gift rather than a binding attachment to the physical item. The sentiment of gratitude centers on the giver, not the object itself. This perspective highlights the intrinsic connection between gratitude and the giver's thoughtfulness.

The author's advice covers a wide spectrum—from practical organization methods to the emotional intricacies of parting with sentimental items. The importance of narratives and stories, along with the items, is a focal point.

If you possess a gift given to you years ago but now finds no utility in your life, remember not to carry the burden of guilt for no longer needing or using it. The connection forged with the gift occurred when it was given, and passing it on to someone else establishes a new connection devoid of guilt. This recurring theme of releasing possessions while retaining mental and physical energy is a cornerstone of the author's message. She encourages the act of letting go while still present, fostering connections with belongings and memories.

If you cannot find a recipient for your possessions, consider selling them and donating the proceeds to charity. Without proactive downsizing, one's cherished belongings might be relegated to an auction or even a landfill, which benefits no one except the auction house.

Consider recording stories while sorting through possessions. This technique could involve writing them down or capturing them on video, not necessarily for publication, but as a therapeutic means of processing emotions while navigating belongings. This introspective storytelling mirrors the author's approach in the book and can offer a cathartic avenue during the process.

In her concluding thoughts, the author conveys her aim to propel readers into action, providing a positive perspective on the hours saved by streamlining possessions. This thoughtful downsizing not only simplifies one's life but also relieves loved ones of the future responsibility of managing unwanted belongings. The book encapsulates the author's desire to inspire others to embark on their own "death cleaning" journey and ultimately share the benefits of a clutter-free life with those around them.

Self-Reflection Questions

- *What Are My Motivations?*

Take a moment to reflect on why you are considering downsizing and decluttering. What are the driving forces behind this decision?

- *What Possessions Truly Matter?*

Look around your living space and identify items with genuine value and significance. Consider the stories, memories, or practical uses associated with these items.

- *How Will Downsizing Improve My Life?*

Envision the positive outcomes of a clutter-free and organized living space. How will downsizing impact your daily life, mental well-being, and relationships?

Exercises

- *Daily Gratitude Journal*

Dedicate a small notebook section as your "Downsizing Gratitude Journal." Daily, write down three items you are grateful for in your life. These items could be possessions, experiences, or even personal qualities. Use this journal as a reminder of the value you already have.

- *Item Reflection Challenge*

Choose an item you've been hesitant to let go of. Write a paragraph reflecting on the memories associated with it and the emotions it brings up. Then, imagine someone else benefiting from the item and write a few sentences about how it could enhance their life.

Personal Notes

Chapter 2: Swedish Death Cleaning Vs. Conventional Decluttering

The Swedish death cleaning technique has gained considerable popularity recently. Let's briefly highlight the similarities between Swedish death cleaning and conventional decluttering.

Similarities

- Evaluation of Belongings: Both methods involve a thorough evaluation of one's possessions, emphasizing the understanding that items are, fundamentally, just objects.

- Sense of Lightness: Swedish death cleaning and standard decluttering provide a sense of liberation, akin to a weight being lifted. Clearing away clutter frees up physical space and unburdens the mind.

- Appreciation for Life: Both methods prioritize an appreciation for life. Recognizing the transient nature of existence is a central theme in both approaches.

Differences

One distinct aspect of Swedish death cleaning is its forward-looking perspective, contrasting with the present-focused approach of decluttering. When practicing Swedish death cleaning, the future life of an item is frequently considered while sorting through belongings. This contemplation adds a unique layer to the process.

Furthermore, Swedish death cleaning places a more pronounced emphasis on downsizing and streamlining possessions, often with the intention of easing the burden on loved ones after one's passing. The method encourages individuals to thoughtfully distribute their belongings to prevent leaving an overwhelming task for their family and friends. In contrast, standard decluttering primarily centers on creating a harmonious living environment in the present. The goal is to cultivate a space that aligns with your immediate needs and preferences without the overarching consideration of future events.

Indeed, we're encouraged to pose a pivotal question during the process: "Would anyone derive greater happiness if I were to retain this item?" This forward-looking perspective, focusing on the future when our loved ones, friends, and family lay eyes on these possessions, guides our decision-making. This question consistently resonates as we sift through what to retain and what to part with throughout the Swedish death cleaning journey.

Central to this method is confronting our mortality – anything left behind can inadvertently erect emotional barriers for our dear ones, hindering their progression through grief. This underscores our contemplation of the interactions these items will foster after our passing.

Undoubtedly, this lens adds complexity to decluttering. It surpasses evaluating the present appeal of an item and delves into the intricate realm of others' emotions and future perceptions. The process necessitates meticulousness and thoughtfulness, thus naturally extending its duration. A comprehensive Swedish death clean, involving a thorough assessment of all belongings, can indeed span years.

Swedish death cleaning tends to be infused with heightened emotion compared to standard decluttering. Swift decluttering sessions typically apply to everyday items like discarded papers or broken objects. Swift decisions are made because we're willing to relinquish many of them when overwhelmed by excessive possessions without much deliberation. Contemplation isn't requisite for retaining a kitchen spatula or extra bathroom towels; these choices can be swift and straightforward.

Yet, these two methods significantly converge within the realm of sentimentality. This juncture is the core of Swedish death cleaning, predominantly manifesting when we encounter sentimental items. These items encompass treasured possessions with potential generational significance. Here, the divergence between standard decluttering and Swedish death cleaning diminishes.

The differentiation emerges when we face these sentimental possessions. Take, for instance, a wedding dress. Standard decluttering might prompt the question, "Do I still derive joy from this dress?" and the decision-making process is relatively swift. However, Swedish death cleaning introduces a layer of emotion. The query evolves into a deeper exploration, intertwining memories and evoking emotional ties. It evolves into, "Would retaining this dress make someone else happier?" This emotional weight amplifies the decision-making process.

The essence of Swedish death cleaning resonates here—its heart lies in these emotionally charged decisions. The profound attachment to these special items intensifies the emotional connection, prompting contemplation about how future generations will perceive and cherish these treasures. The possibility of sentimental legacies stirs our emotions, making it challenging to part with items that encapsulate personal histories.

Once again, the Swedish death cleaning method evokes a deeper emotional connection with our belongings. This emotional resonance particularly centers around the sentimental items—the heart of Swedish death cleaning. As a result, this method fosters more of a communal, connected process compared to the relatively individual nature of standard decluttering.

In the Swedish death cleaning approach, decisions often revolve around passing down or gifting items, transforming the process into a more interactive endeavor. This may involve reaching out to friends or family members to inquire if they'd like to inherit certain possessions or receive particular gifts before our passing. This interactive dynamic can lead to sharing stories behind these items, adding a layer of personal significance. The connection between the giver and recipient deepens through conversations or notes accompanying the items.

Conversely, standard decluttering is often a solitary journey down memory lane. The rediscovery of items, like a dress worn at a memorable event, triggers personal reflection and nostalgia. Yet, in Swedish death cleaning, the focus expands beyond oneself, encompassing the item's significance to the individual and its potential value to others.

Swedish death cleaning was traditionally undertaken around the age of 65 or beyond, a cultural norm. At this stage, accumulating possessions over the years can become overwhelming. This often necessitates involving a partner, family member, or friend to navigate the process alongside you. This shared experience brings shared emotions—laughter and tears—turning the decluttering ordeal into a more cohesive and supportive endeavor. This focus on connection is intrinsically woven into the process, designed to ease the emotional and logistical burden of sorting through years of memories.

An essential distinction lies in the sense of finality that Swedish death cleaning brings compared to standard decluttering. In standard decluttering, the assurance of being able to replace items somewhat mitigates the regret of discarding them. Should we later regret parting with a pair of jeans, finding a new pair is a relatively straightforward task. However, Swedish death cleaning often prompts a "one-and-done" perspective. Given its emotional intensity, exhaustive nature, and profound implications, people embarking on this method lean towards a more decisive approach. While replacement remains an option, the emotional weight encourages a more definitive mindset. The aim is to avoid revisiting the same items in a few years, faced with the same decisions and emotional strain.

Moreover, it's noticeable that people tend to approach Swedish death cleaning with a more comprehensive mindset than they might adopt for standard decluttering. The inclination is to delve into every cabinet, explore each storage area, and scrutinize every item. This meticulous attention stems from the desire to evaluate every possession thoroughly. In a Swedish death clean, decisions extend beyond mere discarding; they encompass considerations about potential beneficiaries if an item is to be passed down. Some individuals even contemplate gifting items to their intended recipients while they are still living. This approach's depth and involvement create a thorough and thoughtful decluttering process.

The deliberate, unhurried manner of Swedish death cleaning contributes to a profound appreciation of the outcome. This method instills a sense of accomplishment for the present and future. The satisfaction derived from enjoying clutter-free spaces during one's lifetime and sparing loved ones the burden of dealing with an excess of belongings after one's passing is a point of pride. This measured approach likely also fosters a more lasting outcome, as the exhaustive nature of Swedish death cleaning, spanning potentially years, underscores the intention of addressing clutter comprehensively—aiming for a one-time endeavor.

While Swedish death cleaning and standard decluttering exhibit differences, it's important not to label one superior. These approaches represent distinct paths to managing belongings. Benefits are evident when opting for an immersive Swedish death clean or adhering to the more conventional decluttering route. Both methods lead to a liberation from excess, creating open spaces for living and thinking.

In the end, the choice between these methods rests on individual preferences, circumstances, and goals. Regardless of the approach chosen, the outcome is an unburdened space, both physically and mentally—a transformation that enhances daily life and offers a meaningful contribution to the future.

Personal Notes

Chapter 3: The Secrets to Successful Decluttering and Organization

The insights I'm about to share may seem like common sense, but the challenge lies in how these concepts are frequently misconstrued or misunderstood. Such misconceptions can sow anxiety or reluctance when embarking on decluttering or organizing. I aim to dispel these misunderstandings and provide clear guidance to pave the way for success in your pursuit.

Differentiating Between Decluttering and Organizing

These two concepts are often conflated, leading to frustration when attempted simultaneously. The truth is, while they are interconnected, they serve distinct purposes. Decluttering involves the intentional removal of excess—both physical possessions that encroach on our spaces and the commitments that consume our time. The goal is to pare down to a manageable level, establishing a foundation. Once decluttering has occurred, the stage is set for organizing—a process that involves finding designated places for retained items and devising systems that facilitate seamless living. These processes are symbiotic, yet decluttering must precede organizing to establish an effective order.

The Personal Nature of Clutter

Clutter is a personal discomfort. This adjective 'personal' is pivotal, as it underscores the variation in how clutter affects individuals. What feels overwhelming and burdensome to one may not hold the same weight for another. Hence, whether a space appears cluttered is subjective and dependent on its impact. What transforms clutter into clutter is the emotional burden it imposes. Herein lies the significance: Decluttering is a personal journey tailored to one's feelings and experiences.

Attempting to impose your perspective on others' clutter is counterproductive. Whether it's advising your aunty or discussing it with your spouse, respect the individual nature of this experience. Your feelings and perceptions are within your control. If your surroundings and belongings generate discomfort, embarking on a decluttering journey could be beneficial. As you gain mastery over your own clutter, others might seek your guidance. Until then, comprehend that this is a personal voyage driven by personal discomfort.

The Time Myth in Decluttering

There is a misconception that decluttering must occur swiftly. This fallacy circulates widely within decluttering and organizing discussions, largely due to the instinct to rid ourselves of overwhelming clutter as rapidly as possible. However, the reality is that decluttering necessitates time—an amount that varies among individuals. Some may deliberate over every item, leading to a slower pace. Others might confront clutter head-on, which can expedite the process. Perhaps you're the type who enjoys gamifying the experience, engaging in methods like the minimalism game or a timed session using a laundry basket. Both of these approaches can be enjoyable and effective. The key is that your chosen pace is the right pace for you. Avoid pushing yourself to rush through solely because of an assumed need for speed. The pace that suits you, whether it's tackling a whole room on a weekend or a single drawer at a time, is entirely valid.

The Power of Choice in Creating Clutter-Free Spaces

Clutter results from choices—choices we've made. This can be a tough reality to accept, acknowledging that the burden and frustration we feel stem from past decisions. These decisions include buying unnecessary or unused items and holding onto possessions far longer than necessary. Gradually, these choices accumulate, leading to a point where the clutter becomes unmanageable. It can be a challenging realization, yet it's not meant to shame anyone. Instead, it's an opportunity to gain perspective and foster healthier decision-making moving forward. The aim isn't to cast blame but to recognize that the clutter we face originates from choices. Acknowledging this empowers us to make more mindful decisions as we move ahead.

Adapting Organizing Systems to Life's Changes

Organizing systems must adapt. This truth can be disheartening for those who feel that after diligently decluttering and establishing effective organizing systems, the hard work should result in perpetual smooth sailing and a perpetually clutter-free existence.

Unfortunately, this isn't quite the case due to the ever-changing nature of our lives. With evolving schedules, growing children, shifting jobs, and various other developments, our organizing systems must grow and adapt to keep pace with these changes. It's natural for systems to shift to accommodate these shifts—a healthy sign of adaptability. Recognizing this need for evolution is key, as our lives are dynamic, and our systems should be as well. So, rest assured, it's not about perfecting a system and being done with it forever; it's about acknowledging the need to adjust and refine as life progresses.

Boundaries for a Clutter-Free Life

Organizing plays a pivotal role in maintaining clutter-free spaces. In particular, I'm referring to the container method of organizing, which entails setting clear boundaries or limits on the number of items we keep. This practice remarkably effectively preserves a healthy inventory level within our homes and lives. When you consider your living space, you'll notice various built-in containers—closets, cabinets, and drawers. Additionally, there are standalone containers designed for this purpose. All these containers inherently possess a capacity limit, and it's essential to honor these limits.

Acknowledging the finite nature of our storage spaces simplifies decision-making. For instance, imagine spotting a piece of clothing you adore in a store. However, a choice must be made upon recognizing that your closet—your clothing container—is already brimming at maximum capacity. You must decide whether to part with an item in your closet to make room for the new piece or to leave the new item behind due to space constraints. This approach removes much of the emotional struggle from the equation. You're committed to maintaining each container at its limit, promoting an organized, clutter-free environment.

Embracing Imperfection

There is a misconception that a flawlessly decluttered and organized home is attainable. In reality, this notion is far from the truth. Striving for an unattainable ideal during the decluttering and organizing process is misguided. Setting your sights on an unrealistic standard merely leads to a futile pursuit, as the polished images on Instagram. There will be days of busyness, illness, unexpected clutter, and instances when organizing systems cease to function optimally. The perpetual state of perfect tidiness and order is an illusion. It's important to recognize that these glimpses of perfection are just that—glimpses. They aren't the norm, and it's crucial not to set unattainable expectations that can immobilize you.

The allure of perfection can breed fear and paralysis, deterring individuals from even attempting the journey of decluttering and organizing. I encourage you to embrace progress over perfection. The essence of this endeavor lies in incremental steps tailored to your unique needs and circumstances. It's about establishing a level of inventory that suits you and your family and identifying organizing systems that enhance the flow of your life. Your version of perfection should be grounded in what resonates with you—not what conforms to external standards.

Remember, the journey of decluttering and organizing is inherently imperfect. It's about navigating your path, discovering what resonates with you, and finding your equilibrium. It's not about comparing yourself to others or aspiring to unrealistic ideals. Your journey is distinct, and the pursuit of progress is the essence.

Self-Reflection Questions

- *What Misconceptions Have I Held About Decluttering and Organizing?*

Reflect on any preconceived notions or misunderstandings you've had about the decluttering and organizing process. How have these misconceptions influenced your approach to creating a clutter-free, organized space?

- *How Can I Embrace Imperfection in the Decluttering Journey?*

Consider your expectations for a clutter-free and organized home. Are you striving for an unattainable standard of perfection?

How can you shift your perspective to embrace progress over perfection and find contentment in your unique journey?

Exercises

- *Personalized Decluttering Approach*

Write a list of the past misconceptions you've held about decluttering and organizing. Beside each misconception, jot down a new, more accurate understanding that you've gained from this chapter. Use these insights to craft a personalized approach to decluttering and organizing that aligns with your newfound clarity.

- *Progress over Perfection Manifesto*

Create a "Progress over Perfection Manifesto" as a visual reminder of your commitment to embracing imperfection in your decluttering and organizing journey. Incorporate phrases and affirmations that resonate with you, celebrating the value of progress, adaptability, and your unique path. Display this manifesto in a place where you'll see it regularly for encouragement.

Personal Notes

Chapter 4: Three Key Steps for Effective Life Organization

Fortunately, I've discovered that a few simple practices can significantly enhance my clarity about life and its demands. I'll break this down into three key steps.

Illuminating Insights

I've realized the importance of gaining a clear perspective to organize my life effectively. It surprises me how few individuals actually undertake this process. There's an unparalleled sense of achievement in creating distance between the thoughts swirling in your mind and the external world by jotting them down or sketching them out.

Notepads are an absolute treasure for organizing thoughts. However, a journal or digital tools can serve the purpose if that suits your preference. The paramount aspect is consolidating all your ideas in one designated place. Disorganization in where you record these thoughts might lead to losing valuable insights. I'm an ardent advocate of analog methods—pen and paper, specifically. In my opinion, no productivity app or software comes close to the sheer power of these traditional tools. The tactile sensation of scribbling and structuring ideas is truly gratifying.

Another critical factor to consider: whenever your phone or computer is within reach, so are distractions, merely two clicks away. It's not your fault if a brilliant idea leads you to your phone and then to a notification, spiraling into watching a random video. This phenomenon is intentionally designed. Allow yourself a change of pace and switch to the old-school approach. Trust me, it's worth the effort.

It's absolutely normal not to have a clear vision of your future. Life and the world are tumultuous, and it's natural for this initial stage to be somewhat chaotic. Embracing this chaos is more productive than resisting it. Order will naturally emerge, often through the process of refining your thoughts. I engage in multiple iterations, redrawing and rewriting my concepts until they're crystal clear. The crux here is acknowledging the potency of externalizing your thoughts rather than allowing them to remain confined within your mind.

A skill I observe many lack is the capacity to externalize their ideas—bringing their mental constructs into the tangible realm. And this is precisely where everything starts.

Strategic Focus

I frequently emphasize two finite resources we all possess: time and attention. These precious commodities demand our thoughtful engagement. With limitations in these resources, the need for prioritization becomes paramount. It's an inescapable fact: you can't do everything. While I often wish for a multitude of lives to fulfill my aspirations, the reality is that I have this singular existence. The optimal course of action, then, is to maximize what I have.

Numerous approaches exist to tackle prioritization. A concept that recently caught my attention is the Eisenhower Matrix, popularized by former President Eisenhower. He categorized tasks based on their importance and urgency. This method's value transcends the tool itself. It's about cultivating a mindset that distinguishes essential tasks from those that can be deferred. Surprisingly, my favored method for this process is conversation.

Conversations are undervalued in many respects. I consistently glean immense value when I share ideas with others. While I ultimately make decisions regarding my priorities and resource allocation, external perspectives offer a valuable counterbalance. I've recognized my tendency to harbor unrealistic expectations about what I can achieve in a given timeframe. Having individuals who provide a reality check is immensely beneficial. I've found that the most constructive discussions come from those you respect—people who have faith in you but are unafraid to provide honest feedback.

The Temporal Scope

A critical insight emerged through personal experimentation with self-organization: I struggle to envision my life beyond three months. My effective planning horizon seems closer to two and a half months, though three months serves as a manageable benchmark. It equates to a quarter of a year—90 days—a span offering substantial progress potential without becoming overwhelming. Within this window, even incremental progress is discernible.

I transcribe my jotted notes and chaotic brainstorming from step one into a tangible, hand-drawn timeline. This process incorporates insights from step two, where my priorities have crystallized. This visual representation aids in identifying project sequences, prioritization, and the flow of activities.

Certainly, various methods exist for executing this step. It doesn't necessitate a strict chronological timeline. In the past, I created mood boards as an alternative, encapsulating what I aimed to achieve over the next three months. While reality rarely aligns entirely with our plans, a three-month timeframe empowers focused effort toward well-defined objectives.

The three steps are clear:

- First, extricate your ideas from your mind by documenting them—be it writing, scribbling, or listing—fostering a skill that celebrates unfiltered expression.
- Second, grasp the fundamental importance of distinguishing priorities; this is your foundational step toward effective resource allocation.
- Finally, manifest your to-do's, projects, and concepts along a three-month trajectory. A mood board can be a creative alternative if a timeline doesn't resonate.

Self-Reflection Questions

- *How Can I Better Externalize My Thoughts and Ideas?*

Reflect on your current approach to capturing your thoughts and ideas. Are you effectively externalizing them from your mind? What methods could you implement to consolidate and document your insights?

- *What Role Do Conversations Play in My Prioritization Process?*

Consider the value of conversations in your life, particularly regarding prioritization and decision-making. Do you actively discuss with others to gain external perspectives and insights? How can you incorporate more meaningful conversations into your process of strategic focus?

Exercises

- *Mind-to-Paper Transition*

Reflect on the ways you currently capture your thoughts and ideas. Do you find them scattered or confined within your mind? Choose a method (e.g., writing, sketching, listing) to consolidate and externalize your thoughts. Commit to using this method consistently and designate a specific place to store these documented insights.

- *Conversational Reflection*

Identify individuals in your life whose perspectives you value and respect. These could be friends, mentors, colleagues, or family members. Write down their names and consider how you can engage in meaningful conversations with them to gain insights into your priorities and resource allocation.

<u>Personal Notes</u>

Chapter 5: Step-by-Step Guide to Swedish Death Cleaning

Step 1: Set Your Intentions

Swedish Death Cleaning is not a morbid or negative task. It's a way to take control of your belongings, your living space, and your legacy. Recognize that you're creating a more organized and meaningful environment for yourself and those who will eventually manage your belongings.

Reflect on Your Belongings

- Begin by reflecting on the items you own. Consider what truly adds value, meaning, and joy to your life.

- Think about whether certain possessions represent your passions, experiences, or memories or if they've simply become clutter.

Embrace Mindfulness

- As you browse through your belongings, cultivate a sense of mindfulness. Take note of your emotional reactions to various items.
- Recognize that giving up stuff does not imply giving up memories; rather, it is about cherishing the substance of those memories.

Clarify Your Priorities

- Consider what matters most to you at this stage of your life. Are there possessions that align with your current values and goals?
- Determine what you want your living space to represent: a place of tranquility, functionality, and reflection.

Envision the Future

- Imagine the relief your loved ones might feel when they don't have to deal with overwhelming clutter and possessions of unclear significance.

- Visualize the space you'll create by letting go of unnecessary items, allowing you to focus on what truly matters.

Reduce Decision-Making for Others

- Recognize that the Swedish Death Cleaning process is a thoughtful deed. You're making decisions on your own terms, removing the burden off your loved ones of making these decisions during a difficult time.

Embrace the Opportunity

- View Swedish Death Cleaning as an opportunity to curate your life's possessions and leave an intentional and meaningful legacy behind.

- Embrace the sense of empowerment from taking charge of your surroundings and your story.

By setting clear intentions and understanding the significance of Swedish Death Cleaning, you lay the foundation for a purposeful and thoughtful journey through the decluttering process. This mindset will guide you as you navigate each step and make decisions about the items that have been a part of your life's journey.

Step 2: Start Early

Swedish Death Cleaning is a time-consuming process that should be approached progressively. Starting early allows you to approach the task more carefully and deliberately. Allowing yourself enough time allows you to make well-considered decisions concerning your belongings without feeling overwhelmed.

Plan Regular Sessions

- Set aside a particular time for Swedish Death Cleaning. This could be a few hours per week or one day each month.
- Consistency is essential for making steady progress while not feeling burdened.

Focus on Categories

- Divide your possessions into clothing, books, documents, sentimental items, and more categories.
- Concentrate on one category at a time to prevent feeling overwhelmed.

Prioritize Sentimental Items

- Before going on to sentimental objects, start with less emotionally charged categories, as these can take more time and emotional energy to sort through.

Reflect and Reevaluate

- Starting early allows you to digest the emotions associated with different items gradually.
- You can revisit nostalgic items over time, allowing yourself to process the feelings connected with letting go.

Avoid Decision Fatigue

- Making a large number of decisions in a short span can lead to decision fatigue.

- Spacing out the process reduces the mental strain of making numerous choices about your belongings.

Starting early with Swedish Death Cleaning lets you approach the task calmly and intentionally. By dedicating regular, focused time to the process, you ensure that you make well-thought-out decisions that reflect your values and desires, both for your living space and your legacy.

Step 3: Categorize Possessions

Categorizing your belongings is a crucial phase in the Swedish Death Cleaning method. It allows you to divide the task into manageable chunks, making it simpler to make decisions and stay organized. By concentrating on one category at a time, you can declutter with greater efficiency and consideration.

Identify Categories

- Separate your possessions into distinct categories. Clothing, books, documents, sentimental items, household items, and electronics are common categories.

Tackle One Category at a Time

- Start with one category to avoid becoming inundated. This targeted approach enables you to give each item the attention it deserves.

Gather Items from Each Category

- Collect all items from the selected category and position them in the designated area for sorting. This visual representation illustrates the extent of your possessions.

Evaluate Each Item

- Evaluate the importance and relevance of each item in the category to your existence.
- Consider whether the item offers pleasure, is useful, or has sentimental value.

Sort into Keep, Donate/Sell, and Discard Piles

- Create three distinct piles for each category: items to retain, sell or donate, and throw away.
- Be practical and truthful in your decision-making, focusing on what genuinely corresponds to your current life stage.

Consider the 80/20 Rule

- Apply the 80/20 rule, recognizing that you most likely utilize 20% of your belongings 80% of the time.
- Prioritize the 20% of your possessions that contribute most to your life and well-being.

Assess Storage Space

- Consider the available storage space in your residence as you declutter.
- This knowledge can help you decide what to keep, ensuring you don't keep more than your space can adequately accommodate.

Repeat the Procedure

- After completing one category, proceed to the next.
- As you declutter your belongings, your sense of accomplishment will increase.

Categorizing your belongings simplifies the decision-making process and prevents you from feeling overwhelmed by the prospect of decluttering your entire space at once. By tackling one category at a time, you can devote your time and energy to making deliberate decisions about each item, resulting in a more organized and purposeful living space.

Step 4: Assess Each Item

Assessing every item is essential to Swedish Death Cleaning. It is a method that assists you in determining the true value and significance of your possessions. By evaluating each item, you can make informed judgments regarding what to keep, what to discard, and what has sentimental value.

Ask Meaningful Questions

- Ask yourself about each item, "Does this item still serve a purpose in my life?" Does it make me happy or improve my well-being?
- Consider the item's compatibility with your current objectives, lifestyle, and values.

Sentimental Significance

- For sentimental items, reflect on the memories associated with them.

- Consider if the item truly represents those memories or if a photograph or written record might serve the same purpose.

Frequency of Use

- Think about how often you use or interact with the item. Is it a regular part of your life, or does it stay hidden away?

Emotional Connection

- Gauge your emotional response to the item. It might be worth keeping if it evokes positive emotions or is deeply meaningful.

Be Ruthless Yet Thoughtful

- Be willing to let go of items that no longer hold value or serve a purpose in your life.
- Remember that by discarding what you no longer need, you're creating space for what truly matters.

Swedish Death Cleaning prompts you to contemplate your legacy. Rather than hoarding objects merely for their material value, prioritize those that will convey your essence and story.

Assessing each item lets you make decisions congruent with your Swedish Death Cleaning objectives. By assessing your belongings' significance, sentimentality, and utility, you can create a more purposeful living space and ensure that the items you keep have genuine value in your life's journey.

Step 5: Keep, Donate, Discard

The categorization of your belongings into "Keep," "Donate/Sell," and "Discard" categories is a crucial aspect of Swedish Death Cleaning. This step lets you make deliberate decisions regarding what to retain, what can benefit others, and what is no longer useful. By organizing items into these categories, you curate your possessions to reflect your current lifestyle and objectives.

Keep

- Choose to preserve truly valuable items and bring you joy.

- Prioritize possessions that improve your daily routine, reflect your personality, and support your objectives.

Donate/Sell

- Donate or sell items in good condition that are no longer useful to you.
- Consider making contributions to charities, shelters, and community organizations. Additionally, selling items can generate additional income.

Discard

- Items no longer useful, valuable, or significant must be discarded responsibly.
- Follow local waste disposal guidelines or recycling programs when discarding items.

Avoid the "Someday" Trap:

- Resist the temptation to save items for "someday" that may never arrive.
- Make decisions based on your current requirements and preferences instead of hypothetical future scenarios.

<u>Repeat for Each Category</u>

- Apply the keep-donate-throw-away method to each decluttering category of belongings.
- To create a well-balanced living space, maintain consistency in your decision-making.

<u>Reevaluate Regularly</u>

- Periodically examine the items you've chosen to retain as you progress through Swedish Death Cleaning.
- Ensure your decisions continue to reflect your shifting priorities.

Organizing your belongings into retain, donate/sell, and discard piles enables you to gain control over your possessions and intentionally shape your living space. You are constructing a living environment that reflects your values, reduces clutter, and positively impacts your life and the lives of your loved ones by making mindful decisions.

Step 6: Consider Sentimental Items

Managing sentimental items is frequently one of the most emotionally taxing aspects of Swedish Death

Cleaning. These items contain profound memories and emotions, making decision-making more difficult. However, approaching sentimental items carefully can help you successfully navigate this step.

Prioritize Meaningful Experiences

- Focus on preserving the items with the deepest meaning and memories.
- Consider whether the item accurately embodies the memory you wish to preserve.

Restriction of Quantity

- Despite the importance of sentiment, consider whether keeping every sentimental item is necessary.
- Select a few elements that are representative of a variety of memories.

Preserve electronically

- Frequently, photographs, correspondence, and documents can be digitally preserved.
- Consider photographing or scanning items to create a digital archive and reduce physical debris.

Repurpose versus reuse

- Some objects can be repurposed or remade into something useful.
- For instance, the fabric from sentimental apparel could be used to create a quilt or a work of art.

Address Guilt and Responsibility

- Don't hold on to sentimental objects out of remorse or obligation.
- Recognize that your sentiments toward a particular item may differ from those of others.

Think About the Future

- Consider whether your loved ones will find these sentimental items valuable after your passing.
- Choose items that will meaningfully continue on your legacy.

Dealing with sentimental items necessitates striking a delicate balance between respecting the memories they represent and making practical decisions that accord with your current goals and way of life. By approaching these objects with intention, you can create a meaningful connection to the past without compromising the present or your vision for the future.

Step 7: Organize and Label

Organizing and categorizing your possessions is a vital component of Swedish Death Cleaning. This procedure guarantees that your possessions are simply accessible and manageable for you and your loved ones. By establishing a well-organized system, you simplify the administration of your possessions and enhance long-term efficiency.

Develop Storage Options

- Invest in storage options such as boxes, bins, shelving, and cabinets.
- These help keep your possessions organized, neat, and safe.

Group similar objects

- Group similar objects to make them simpler to locate.

- Place kitchen items in one area, books in another, and papers in designated containers.

Utilize Labels

- Clearly label containers and crates with their contents.
- Labels make it simple for you and others to find particular objects.

Give Accessibility Priority

- Keep routinely utilized items within easy reach. This prevents aggravation when browsing for frequently used items.

Think About Long-Term Storage

- If you are storing items for sentimental reasons or future generations, choose methods of storage that will preserve their condition over time.

Reduce Cluttered Spaces

- Ensure surfaces and spaces remain devoid of debris.

- Review and clear out storage areas frequently to prevent accumulation.

Maintain an Inventory or Catalog

- Maintain a physical or digital inventory of your valuable possessions, important documents, and their locations.
- This inventory assists your loved ones in the future administration of your estate.

Provide Instructions

- Attach or include care instructions with products in your inventory if they have them.
- This ensures that your property is well-maintained even after you are no longer responsible for it.

Evaluate and Modify

- Review the organization of your possessions frequently and make necessary adjustments.
- This allows you to maintain an effective system that meets your evolving requirements.

Organizing and designating your belongings simplifies your living space and makes it easier for your loved ones to manage your belongings when the time comes. A well-organized environment demonstrates your attentiveness and care, making passing on your legacy easier and less stressful.

Step 8: Create an Inventory

A practical and considerate aspect of Swedish Death Cleaning is creating an inventory of your valuable possessions and essential documents. This inventory provides a detailed list of your possessions, making it simpler for your loved ones to administer your estate and fulfill your wishes. Gathering this information ensures a smooth transition and reduces the tension associated with managing your affairs.

Document Essential Elements

- Include jewelry, artwork, heirlooms, and significant electronic devices among your valuables.

- Include descriptions, photographs, estimated values, and any pertinent background information.

Organize Critical Documents

- Collect important documents such as wills, trusts, insurance policies, financial accounts, property certificates, and medical records.
- Consider digitizing the hard copies as a backup and keep them in a secure location.

Provide Location Details

- Notate the location of each item and document within your residence.
- Specify which storage containers, chambers, or safes hold various belongings.

Provide Contact Details

- Include the contact information of your attorney, financial advisor, executor, and anyone involved in your estate planning. This ensures your loved ones will know who to contact for guidance.

Share Access Details

- Provide access information if your documents are stored digitally or in password-protected accounts.

- Maintain a secure, up-to-date list of all passwords and access credentials.

Review Frequently

- Maintain a current inventory by periodically examining and updating it. This ensures that all modifications and acquisitions are properly documented.

Communicate the Existence of the Inventory

- Inform your executor, family members, or other trusted individuals of the existence and location of your inventory. This information will be useful when the time arrives to manage your possessions.

Securely store

- Keep physical copies of the inventory in an accessible and secure location.

- Consider preserving a digital copy in a password-protected cloud storage service or on a password-protected drive.

Creating an inventory is an act of foresight that can alleviate the tension of a difficult time for your loved ones. It demonstrates your thoughtfulness and facilitates the execution of your wishes while simplifying the administration of your property and estate.

Step 9: Review Regularly

Reviewing your possessions and decisions made during Swedish Death Cleaning regularly is a practical and ongoing aspect of the process. This step ensures that your living space remains organized, your goals remain current, and your belongings continue to reflect your current lifestyle. You can maintain a clutter-free environment and make necessary adjustments by periodically reviewing your decisions.

Schedule Periodic Evaluations

- Establish specific intervals for revisiting your possessions, such as every six months or once a year.
- Regular evaluations prevent clutter from reaccumulating and enable you to assess preference changes.

Evaluate Value and Significance

- Reevaluate the items you've chosen to keep during each inspection.
- Consider whether they continue to bring you pleasure, serve a function, or hold sentimental value.

Adjust as Necessary

- Be receptive to modifying your decisions in response to changes in your life circumstances or priorities.
- Your requirements and preferences may change over time, and so should your possessions.

Describe New Acquisitions

- If you've acquired new items since your last inventory, determine how they work in your current organization system.
- Ensure that these acquisitions align with your established values and goals.

Accept Minimalism

- Utilize periodic evaluations to reaffirm your commitment to minimalism and intentional living.
- Relinquish possessions that no longer add value to your life.

Evaluate Progress

- Each review enables you to assess your progress in decluttering your living space.
- Honor your achievements and their positive influence on your daily existence.

Plan Forward

- Consider how your possessions and choices may change over the next few years.
- Adjust your plans to accommodate alterations to your living situation or future requirements.

Reviewing your possessions frequently ensures that your living environment remains consistent with your aims and values. You make deliberate decisions by remaining proactive and adaptable, leading to a more organized, meaningful, and clutter-free space.

Personal Notes

Chapter 6: Mastering Rapid Decluttering

60-Second Purge

If you are overwhelmed by the clutter in your home and have no clue where to begin, this technique is tailored for you.

- Grab a box or bin – anything at hand will do. This isn't about planning or meticulous organization but swift action.

- With your box or bag in hand, roam around your home and sweep up items you no longer need.

- Get a little messy – swipe things off shelves, clear countertops, open drawers, and pull out anything surplus to requirements.

These are quick decisions; just toss them into the garbage bag. This process won't devour much time, but you'll witness the clutter vanishing before your eyes.

Targeting high-traffic areas

Often, our focus rests on decluttering spaces like closets, attics, or basements – all necessary endeavors, but they might not immediately make your home feel clutter-free. Concentrate on high-traffic areas to swiftly declutter and attain that sense of accomplishment. These are the spaces that catch your eye as you step into your home after a long day's work – the entryway, kitchen, or dining room, for example. The stress and unease you feel upon encountering these eyesores can be overwhelming. To experience rapid and tangible decluttering success, shift your attention to these high-traffic zones.

- Begin by identifying the areas that experience the most foot traffic. You can rank them based on priority.

- Tackle one high-traffic area each day to streamline the decluttering process.
- In each area, scrutinize every item and decide whether to discard, donate, sell, or keep it.

Always remember the cardinal rule of decluttering and organization: every item must have a designated home. Your decluttering efforts will result in a sense of accomplishment and cleanliness. However, maintaining this clutter-free state requires those items to find their designated homes.

Prevent the recurrence of clutter by introducing small but impactful changes. Instead of leaving mail on the dining table, designate a mail caddy. Replace the habit of tossing coats onto the couch with a few hooks in your entryway. These modest adjustments go a long way in preventing clutter from resurfacing. The key is ensuring every item in your space has a purposeful place to return to. This will turn your initial victory into an enduring triumph over clutter.

The Atomic Method

Think of it as a thorough spring cleaning where you roll up your sleeves and tackle the entire house. Apply the same tenacity to decluttering – no scrutinizing each item to decide whether it stays or goes. Avoid getting bogged down in deliberation; be resolute in your approach. Go through your house and clear out everything you don't need. You might dispose of something you could use a month from now, but if swift decluttering is your aim, this is the path to follow.

If you seek a more strategic route, consider crafting a simplified plan. Your objective is swift decluttering, so keep the plan straightforward. Skip over the creation, refinement, and assessment of the plan itself. Focus solely on its execution.

The cardinal rule for decluttering rapidly is: don't halt. I know the fatigue that sets in as you declutter; the desire to wrap it up is strong. However, maintain your momentum. Remember that the "you" a week from now will be immensely grateful. Don't quit; continue steadily decluttering one area after another. Before you realize it, your home will be freed from clutter.

Enlist help from others

If necessary, use a little persuasion to get them on board – invite your kids, friends, or partner. Devise a simple schedule, allocating areas of the home for each person to declutter. More hands mean faster progress. Perfection might not be attainable, but you'll certainly rid your space of substantial clutter.

When delegating tasks, consider using labeled boxes. Designate categories like "toss," "keep," "sell," and "donate." As others declutter, they can sort items into the appropriate boxes. Later, you can review the contents of each box to ensure proper distribution. Few things are as rewarding as this teamwork-driven approach.

Tackling Surface Clutter

Another rapid decluttering method involves tackling surface clutter. These seemingly insignificant items make your space look more cluttered than it is. Random papers on nightstands, desks, dining tables, kitchen counters, and items yet to find their proper places contribute to the visual chaos.

Looking to conquer surface clutter? The optimal approach involves systematically moving from one surface to another, eliminating unnecessary items. If you're keen on expediting the process, consider adopting an Atomic approach – simply sweep items into a box or bin. This technique yields substantial impact; it's the essence of effective tidying.

Forming Habits

Maintaining a clutter-free home hinges on forming habits, and one of the most potent habits is tidying up at day's end. I make it a practice to tidy before leaving any room. This practice ensures my home consistently appears clean and uncluttered. Instead of the common approach of dedicating hours on Sundays to cleaning, tidying up nightly prevents clutter from accumulating and contributes to a positive mindset upon waking.

The "Bag a Day" Strategy

Each day, commit to filling a bag – one for garbage and another for donations. Even if you sustain this habit for just a week, you'll observe clutter gradually dissipating. Avoid letting bags of garbage or donations linger in your living space or car. Dedicate yourself to the process: dispose of the bag of garbage and donate the bag of items swiftly.

Opt for donation or disposal over selling

Selling items demands time and effort. While it's understandable that you might wish to sell certain items, if your primary goal is swift decluttering, consider that items awaiting sale could be stored elsewhere, out of sight. If you possess a basement or garage, these could serve as temporary storage. But to promptly achieve a clutter-free home, prioritize donating or trashing items. These avenues facilitate a faster departure of clutter from your living space.

Halt your buying habits

If you've decluttered your space and experienced the joy of a clutter-free environment, only to find the clutter creeping back a month later, you'll resonate with this point. I'm not advocating for becoming an extreme minimalist, but if your aim is sustained clutter-free living, you need a balance where more items exit than enter.

For many of us, shopping is a beloved activity. After decluttering, when the home is pristine and orderly, the temptation arises. Thoughts like, "Maybe that trinket would add a nice touch," or "A new knife set would be great," might occur. The desire to indulge is natural, but be conscious of what you bring into your home.

Be especially mindful of your spending habits. This mindfulness not only prevents unnecessary purchases but also saves you money. Often, we buy things on impulse that end up having no true purpose in our lives. When the urge to shop strikes, pause and question: Do I genuinely need this? Does it serve a function? Will it genuinely enhance my life and living space? If the answer is no, resist the purchase.

Personal Notes

Chapter 7: Effortless Decluttering: Streamline Your Space, 15 Minutes at a Time

I've compiled a list of 30 items you can easily declutter in just 15 minutes a day.

The Kitchen

<u>Containers</u>

First on the list, and probably the simplest, is the quickest thing you can declutter: containers. I'm not talking about all containers, but those worn-out and lidless ones that take up precious space in your cupboards.

<u>Mug collection</u>

Realistically, we only need about two mugs per adult. But if you're like me, you might have accumulated a surplus. These mugs, however cute, often end up overcrowding our drawers.

Expired and unused spices

Yes, spices do have an expiration date. If you haven't used them in a while, it's time to let go.

Old dish towels

Go through your stash and keep only what you actually use.

Condiment packets

Ketchup, mustard, mayo that we stash on the side door of our fridge. While they're meant for emergencies, let's face it, they tend to accumulate and stay there for years. It's time to part ways.

Freezer Food

The best time to tackle this is when your freezer isn't full. Take everything out, quickly assess, and toss what's unrecognizable or unwanted.

Food you simply don't eat

Often, this can be found lurking in the pantry, especially snacks. Give it a quick review and clear out what's not being enjoyed.

Unused or broken appliances

These items take up a lot of space, especially if you're living in a small city apartment.

Excess dishes and bowls

Most of us accumulate far more than we actually need, often for those times when guests come over. Reevaluate your collection and recycle what you don't require.

Reusable bags

We all seem to amass these; over time, they pile up, and some lose their practicality. Quickly sort through them, launder the ones that need it, and bid farewell to the rest.

So, there you have it—a comprehensive list of items you can swiftly declutter from your kitchen in just 15 minutes a day. A clutter-free space awaits!

The Bathroom

What items can you swiftly declutter in this space? Here's a rundown:

Old, grimy towels

It's time to part ways with those old, grimy towels you've washed countless times that still emanate an unpleasant odor and look worn out.

Hair products

There are often products that we no longer use or need.

Old and unused makeup

Yes, makeup does expire. It's time to let go of what you're not using.

Nail polish

You really don't need an extensive color palette. Stick to the five or six shades you use most frequently. Save the vibrant, glittery hues for special occasions when you can get your nails done.

Hair accessories

We tend to accumulate these cute finds from stores, especially those budget-friendly shops. Yet, we often end up dumping them in various places, forgetting about them.

Shower curtains

We sometimes collect these for different reasons— liking a new design or redoing the bathroom. But if you've updated, why hang onto the old ones?

Travel bottles

Despite not traveling much, we tend to accumulate a surplus of these. This is particularly true for ladies.

Perfumes

We all appreciate pleasant scents, and our preferences may change with the seasons. Evaluate your perfume collection, getting rid of scents you no longer enjoy, or that are running low.

Bath toys

Regular decluttering of your child's bath toys is essential.

Beauty Products

While embracing femininity and enhancing our appearance is wonderful, we often amass drawers full of products, many of which we don't even understand. It's time to meticulously review every bottle and cream and eliminate what's unnecessary.

Those are the ten categories of items you can promptly declutter from your bathroom. With each step, you're paving the way for a more organized and refreshing space.

The Closets

Old socks—particularly those that lack a pair

There seems to be some mysterious force in the laundry machine that thrives on sock disappearances. It's time to let go of these lone socks that serve no purpose but to clutter our drawers.

Scarves

Styles shift, and scarves often follow trends or seasons. If you find scarves that have lost their appeal or are no longer in vogue, they're prime candidates for removal from your closet.

Gloves

Does anyone else feel like they're stockpiling gloves every winter? It's similar to grocery shopping when hungry; we end up with far more pairs than necessary. Pare down the collection to a more practical number.

Clothing that no longer fits

This is an entirely common issue, with changes in size or unrealistic weight-loss goals causing us to cling to ill-fitting items. While some pieces might serve as motivation, the majority just take up precious closet space. Remember, we tend to wear 20% of our clothing 80% of the time.

Jewelry

Trends and the allure of certain jewelry pieces come and go. Timeless items should be preserved, but trinket-like pieces that have fallen out of favor can be let go.

Shoes

It's peculiar how we sometimes develop sentimental attachments to footwear, holding onto them for decades. In reality, they often take up considerable room without offering much benefit. Passing on vintage shoes to younger generations isn't as appealing as it might seem. Despite our emotional ties, shoes are among the easiest and quickest things to declutter.

Special occasion outfits

They're often the forgotten 80% of our wardrobe. Before motherhood, the calendar was peppered with weddings, parties, and anniversaries. But as a mom, the frequency of such events dwindles, yet our closets are still packed with dresses and outfits that rarely see the light of day. Many of these pieces might not even fit anymore as we've changed over the years. It's time to say goodbye to these dresses that have served their purpose. Donate, toss, or sell if they're in good condition.

Jackets and coats

Open up your entryway closet and take stock of what's hanging there. Coats that no longer fit you or your children should be reconsidered. Sometimes, we hold on to outerwear that our kids have outgrown, creating unnecessary clutter. These items can find new homes through donations, making space for the essentials.

Underwear with holes

It happens to everyone, and we've all experienced that awkward moment at work. Let's be practical and compassionate to ourselves—underwear with holes deserves to be discarded. It's about making room for items that make us feel good.

Purses

We adore them, and it's easy to accumulate a vast collection. But let's consider this: How many of those purses do we genuinely use? If you have a daytime and a nighttime purse, that's practical. However, it might be time to reassess if you find yourself surrounded by excess purses. Do we really need 25 to 30 purses? They eat up space and contribute to clutter.

Remember, decluttering your living space need not be an overwhelming task. Approach it as a series of small, manageable steps rather than one giant project. I wish you all the best on your journey to decluttering and creating a more organized and serene living environment.

Personal Notes

Conclusion

As you reach the conclusion of this book, you've embarked on a transformative journey that delves deep into the art of decluttering, organization, and the thought-provoking concept of Swedish Death Cleaning. You've explored the psychology behind accumulation, discovered the power of passing on gifts with intention, and learned the gentle yet impactful approach of Swedish Death Cleaning.

You've been guided through three key steps for effective life organization, embracing the wisdom of illuminating insights, strategic focus, and temporal scope. These steps empower you to bridge the gap between thoughts and action, fostering a more organized and purposeful existence.

The comprehensive step-by-step guide to Swedish Death Cleaning equips you with the tools and mindset needed to undertake this transformative process. From setting your intentions to organizing and labeling, you're now prepared to embark on a journey that goes beyond mere possessions—it's a journey that weaves sentimentality, mindfulness, and purpose into every decision you make.

As you take a final look at the journey you've undertaken within these pages, remember that perfection is not the goal. Embrace the imperfections, acknowledge your progress, and celebrate the steps you've taken towards a more organized and clutter-free life.

Share Your Thoughts

We'd love to hear from you! Drop a review and share your takeaways from this book. Your words can inspire and empower others on their own clutter-free journey.

We invite you to share your experience with others. Your insights, challenges, and triumphs can inspire fellow readers on a similar path. Your review will serve as a beacon of encouragement, guiding others as they navigate the world of decluttering and organization.

Thank you for joining us on this enlightening expedition. As you continue your journey, remember that the pursuit of an organized life is a continuous, evolving process that promises fulfillment, clarity, and freedom.

Good luck!

Personal Notes

Printed in Great Britain
by Amazon

44052565R00066